Michael Mayor

MR TRUMP
GOES TO WASHINGTON

A satirical review of Mr Trump's election
campaign, and his early days in office

Coming soon from Belvedere Publishing:
Harry & His GrownUps

You don't have to pass any exams to become a baby, and yet you are propelled into a world where you are responsible for teaching GrownUps how to become parents.

This book is not written by a doctor or a psychiatrist: instead it comes from the warped mind of someone who was once a baby, and grew up to have babies, and now observes the people around him who make babies and learn to become parents.

Harry & His GrownUps should, first and foremost, make you giggle, but it should also make you think about the challenges of parenting in a new light.

The cute illustrations and simple one-liners make this a book you can easily read in-between cleaning up sick, disposing of smelly nappies, or doing the tenth load of washing.

www.veloce.co.uk
www.hubbleandhattie.co.uk

First published in September 2017 by Veloce Publishing Limited, Veloce House, Parkway Farm Business Park, Middle Farm Way, Poundbury, Dorchester DT1 3AR, England.
Fax 01305 250479 / e-mail info@veloce.co.uk / web www.veloce.co.uk or www.velocebooks.com. ISBN: 978-1-787111-63-9 UPC: 6-36847-01163-5.
British Library Cataloguing in Publication Data – A catalogue record for this book is available from the British Library.
Typesetting, design and page make-up all by Veloce Publishing Ltd on Apple Mac. Printed in India by Replika Press.

Dedication

For Gordon Murray and Brian Cant, the founding fathers of Trumpton,
to whom the author apologises for what he has done

A special thank you to Kate from Shaderlight
for the lovely rendering engine

And a 'yuge' thank you to the good people of
Trumptonshire, without whom the author would
have a life

www.thetrump.co.uk
@Trump_ton
www.facebook.com/TrumptonMayor

Forewords in Four Words

I asked the creator of 'Veep' and 'The Thick of It' to write a foreword for this book;

Hi Mike, that's kind of you to ask but I've just done similar for two other books and I need to stop otherwise I become a book-slut. Apologies, but I'll def tweet about it when it comes out.
All the best, Arm x
Armando Iannucci @Aiannucci

Reeling from this rejection, I turned to the splendid followers of @Trump_ton and asked for a 'Foreword in 4 Words' here are some of the best (and some that paid me bribes) you can see the rest by searching Twitter for the hashtag #MTGTW4words

@LiberalIsland
Art of the steal

Adam Gelfs
Presidenting for Dummies FACT.

Adam Hill @AdamlHill
This just enough words?

Adam Taylor @Kazak1842
BIGLYEST WITCH HUNT EVER

YearsAgroBioDiverse
@AgroBioDiverse
But her emails, right?

Alasdair Heads
May contain fake news!

Andy Elms @aiyeethesquid
There'll be Hell Toupée

Andy Pittman
Mein Covfefe, Trump Diary

Andy Reid
Please open other end

anth_blog @anth_blog
Plausible Deniability on Speed

Ben Gregson @bengregson98
A tremendous book covfefe

Bob Gillham
He WAS the swamp!

Caracal @caracal
Make America Gag Again

Chris Johnson
Great book, the best

Chris Pryor
"Trump's my man" Putin

Clark Campbell
Here are four words

Colin Crooks
I haven't read it

Colin Morley @morley_colin
Make Russia great again

Dale Preece-Kelly
From Tweet to Twit

Dan Russell
President Pence's full back-story

Darren King @DarrenK73
Is this alright mate?

David Church
Somebody hold my tie!

Deb Green @luffdee
Bigly good read. Really

Deb S @Debstar1270
Trumpton keeps me sane

Duncan Browne
Failing fake book! Sad!

Fraser Lovie
Short fingers. Long ties

Gernie Blanston
Lie > Golf > Collude > Repeat

Graeme Francis
All proceeds to me

Helen Walker
100% Fake News Free!

Ian Barber
What a business opportunity.

Jan Shirley
The swamp level rises

Jay Hollis
This'll grab your pussy

Jefo Scrase
Assume the crash position …

John Dexter @JohnDexter51
Finally, some positive Covfefe

John Tomkins @JohnTomkins
From Russia with Love

Jon Meakin @JonMeakinPR
There are no pictures

Judith Blair
When fact met fiction

Justina Juli @justinajuli
The Plot Against America

Kerry M Howells
Fries, ties, spies, lies.

Kevin Murphy
The Presidency for Dummies

Kevin Tolhurst @Tollibolli
Also available in Russian

Kirstie Clegg
Blah blah blah blah

koba1898 @koba1898
Vene vidi vici covfefe

Lindsay Conway
Bigly Book Of Wurds

Marc Elliott de Lama @marcdelliott
Covfefe, Putin & Me

Maria Dalimonte Camilo
Voting in primaries matters

Mark Iliff @markiliff
Unpresidented (thank you Mark)

Mark Laming
It was Obama's fault …

Martin Ballantine @piracycorp
You bought this? Sad

Michelle Benato
You couldn't write it!

Mike Turner @mikerturner
Hair today, impeached tomorrow

Murmeration @matthud59
She got more votes

Nadia Lewis
Tweets from the toilet

ND Kev @kevinfins13
Fake book, good read!

P@ Kent @MagusPerde
Government in 140 characters

Pablo Nazareno
All The President's Lies

Penny Morgan
Make books great again!

Peter Dean
Very, very, VERY sad

Phil Knighton
He came, he tweeted…

Phil Morrow
House of Trump Cards

Philip Grimmer Grimshaw
Vladimir, hold my beer

Philip Thompson
Sponsored by Tie Rack

Pip @Pipsmydog
America duped bigly. Sad.

Redlight @rob_mcivor
Read this and weep

relicta @VamboRools
Tweeting Gets You Everywhere

Rob Shackleton
Trump in Washington Sad!

Robert Branch
It's very very bad

Rory Bell @rorybell73
It's gonna be yuge

Sigrit Hepperle
Show rump, ridicule Trump

Sim Clarke
Where's the golf course?

Simon Morgan
I haven't read it

Sir Donald Flashman
Болтун находка для шпиона

SJL @livesey99
What have you done?

Steg68 @Steg68
Available now on Wikileaks

Steve Bagley @stevebagley
Trumpton Warns America's Trump

Steve Wulfrun
Hilary, be my friend

Steve YATES @sayates
The Very Best Book

Steven Wilson
Always grab life's pussy

Tim Hessey
Donald's Covfefe Table Bookly

Tony Mills
All the best words

Yillie Mycroft
American politics for Dummies.

Yrotitna @yrotitna
The ultimate Presidential heist

In 2016, much to his surprise,
Mr Trump was elected
President of the USA.

This is the story of what
happened when he went to
Washington: the author
does not envisage it
ending well ...

One night a long time ago, Mr Obama (Fake President) told some SAD jokes about Mr Trump, which made him mad

So Mr Trump decided to run for President himself.
Can you see his friend, Vlad, cheering him on?

Once they saw the new plans, Mexico was very happy to pay for Mr Trump's wall

Mr Trump called for a complete ban on Muslims coming to the USA, until he figured out what a Muslim is

Mr Trump created a new game show called
The GOP Debates where he got to choose
names for all the contestants

There is nothing like a war to divert media attention.
So Mr Trump started a war with the media

Mr Trump had no way of telling if any members of his campaign had connections with Russia

Mr Trump asked Mr Pence to join him to attract the LGBT, non-white and non-Christian voters

Mr Trump needed to improve his efficiency,
so he employed Mr Spicer to tell lies for him
while he slept

Mr Trump used his favourite catch-phrase
"Ты уволен!" to get rid of campaign staff
("You're fired!")

As Mr Trump returned from his trip to Mexico, Mr Pence was waiting for him to find out how much they were going to pay for the wall

Border Xing To Mexico

Pussy-Grabber-in-Chief

When lyin' Mrs Clinton
accused Mr Trump of being
a Russian puppet he asked
Mr Putin if this was true

To be honest, nobody was more surprised
at his victory than Mr Trump ...

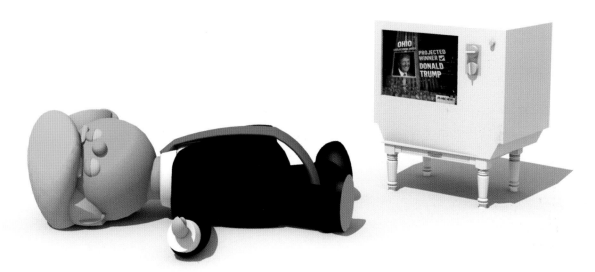

Mr Spicer's first job was to Photoshop a bigger crowd
in the pictures of Mr Trump's inauguration

When someone told Mr Trump the Law of Gravity
was one of Mr Obama's, he repealed it

Mr Trump learned to love the bomb when he
realised that dropping a few distracted
the media for several days

Mr Bannon kept asking Mr Trump to sign
"eggs secutif orders"

Mr Trump had no reason to suspect Mr Flynn, despite the attempts by Mrs Yates to spread #FakeNews

Mrs May took Mr Trump's hand and whispered
"Please stop tweeting all our secrets"

Mr Trump showed Mr Comey his special tape recorder. "I hope there are no tapes," he said

Mr Trump introduced a travel ban,
preventing Melania from
leaving New York

Mr Trump believed that you shouldn't let
your job get in the way of your golf

"You're fired!" said Mr Trump as he got rid
of Mrs Yates for holding a sign

Mr Comey liked to play Hide-and-Seek
with Mr Trump, to stop him being
inappropriate in meetings

Mrs Queen was overseeing the construction of a special golden carriage for Mr Trump's state visit

Mr Trump's friends were really pleased that he didn't behave like a child during his speech to congress

See no evil, hear no evil, tweet some evil

Mr Trump was convinced that Mr Obama
was tapping his microwave

If Mr Trump could just stop the leaks in the
White House, no-one would know he'd
leaked in his bath

Mr Trump refused to shake Mrs Merkel's
hand due to his Germanophobia

In the end, Mr Flynn had to go ... it turned out
that he had Russian connections: who knew?

Mr Trump hoped that Ivanka's
new book had pictures

Mr Trump needed a distraction, so he started a
'Who has the biggest missile' contest with Mr Kim

Every day was Take Your Daughter to Work Day
at the White House

Mr Trump sent his son-in-law to Iraq for some quality time with ISIS, while he planned some quality time with Ivanka

Mr Trump's presidency was more 'Stairgate' than 'Watergate'

Mr Trump had never met, nor colluded with, Mr Trump Jr

Why choose between having a terrific cake and launching missiles against ~~Iraq~~ ~~Iran~~ ~~Syria~~ Covfefe?

It turned out that Mr Trump had sent a
fleet to North Korea in his bathtub only

As her job evolved, Ms Trump
decided to update her latest book

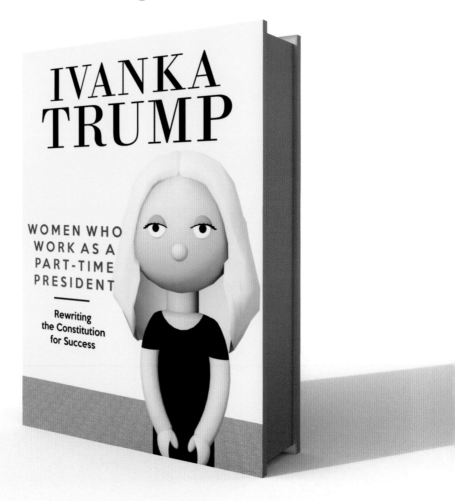

IVANKA
TRUMP

WOMEN WHO
WORK AS A
PART-TIME
PRESIDENT

Rewriting
the Constitution
for Success

After trying the first two buttons, Mr Trump wondered what the 'Nuke'em' button did ...

Mr Trump celebrated his
First 100 Holidays in office!

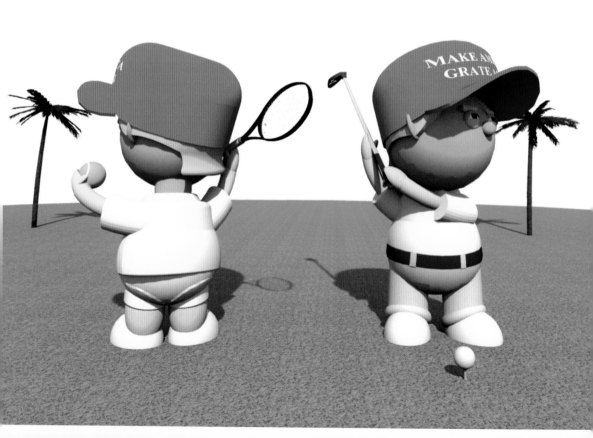

Mr Trump was very pleased with the new phone Mr Putin had sent him as a present

"Hey, Vlad ol' buddy! Fake News says I'm in cahoots with this Mr Putin guy: you ever heard of him?"

"You're fired! and I'll see you in court!" said Mr Trump
"Indeed you will ..." said Mr Comey

Mr Spicer was trying to be more
like the Bush administration

"Stop or I'll Tweet!"

On July 4th we celebrate independence from the
tyranny of being ruled by a rich man who
sat on a golden throne

Mr Trump's plan to build a coal island to offset
the effects of climate change was a real winner!

"My job was to investigate low-life criminals who put the country at risk" said Mr Comey

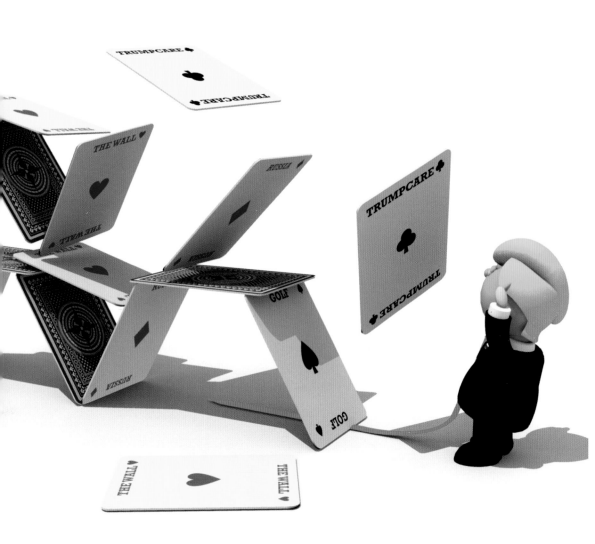

"Tell me the bit of your dream where Trump became President, Michelle – it's too funny"